> *The desire to take medicine is perhaps the greatest feature which distinguishes man from animals.*
> *Sir William Osler, 1849-1919, Canadian physician and founder of modern medicine*

Although many early civilizations took drugs for pleasure, it is unlikely they saw this as a problem. Yet most modern countries regard the increasing use of illegal drugs like cannabis, cocaine, heroin, lysergic acid (LSD), amphetamines and ecstasy as a danger to their society.

> *One teenager in ten has taken LSD. One hundred people have died from taking ecstasy – double previous estimates. This is about the real-life threat facing every family in Britain.*
> *Former UK Prime Minister John Major*

The US has a large number of drug users, particularly among teenagers. In 2000 over 20 per cent of 18-20-year-olds used illegal drugs. In the UK a 2001 survey revealed that over one-third of 15- and 16-year-olds had used marijuana alone.

Many people blame this increase on the attitudes of parents who themselves took drugs when they were young.

> *We have a generation of parents who have a difficult time talking to their kids about drugs, since 57 per cent of them used drugs in the 1960s.*
> *James Copple, US Community Anti-Drugs Coalition*

But it is only relatively recently that governments decided some drugs should be banned. In Britain, until the late 19th century, opium was sold as freely as cigarettes or

▲ *A 19th-century opium den in London's East End. Opium is illegal in the UK today.*

alcohol today; in the US in 1915 there were around 150,000 opium addicts in New York alone. Cocaine was one of the main ingredients of Coca Cola until earlier this century. As doctors gradually became aware of the dangers and addictiveness of drugs like opium and cocaine, many governments made them illegal.

Today the difference between drug use and abuse still largely depends on the attitudes of the society concerned. Most Western countries see alcohol as perfectly acceptable, but in most Islamic nations it is banned. Smoking cigarettes is also seen as acceptable by millions of people – even though cigarettes contain nicotine, a drug which is actually more addictive than heroin.

◀ *Alcohol, nicotine, caffeine and glue are all types of drug.*

Why take illegal drugs?

People take illegal drugs for various reasons. They may be curious to know what effects the drug will have on them, or they may see drug-taking as a way to escape from life or personal problems. But perhaps the main reason is that drugs can bring feelings of pleasure.

▼ *Since the late 1980s, illegal drugs such as ecstasy have become increasingly popular in clubs. Many people enjoy the 'buzz' the drug gives them. It can give users a burst of energy – making them feel that they can dance for hours – as well as feelings of warmth and friendliness towards others.*

" *The vast majority of people who use drugs come to no harm, and many will feel that they have benefited . . . from the relaxation, diversion or temporarily improved social, intellectual or physical performance that can be afforded by some drugs. But there are some very serious risks.* **"**
UK Institute for the Study of Drug Dependence

Ecstasy, for instance, can induce feelings of euphoria, calmness and friendliness, while cocaine makes users feel powerful and energetic, and cannabis brings sensations of relaxation and a greater appreciation of music and food. Other drugs, such as LSD, amphetamines, heroin, magic mushrooms or crack, each have distinct effects of their own. Some users also find pleasure in the fact that what they are doing is illegal.

" *Part of the thrill of drug-taking is that it is illicit. You wouldn't really want to do it with your Mum's blessing.* **"**
Suzanna Moore, The Guardian

But pleasure is not the only reason for taking drugs. Drugs are now part of youth culture, reflected in the music, fashion and language, and many feel pressure from friends to experiment.

Contents

Drug use or abuse? 4

Why take illegal drugs? 6

Are soft drugs really dangerous? 8

Are socially acceptable drugs dangerous? 10

Hurting no one but themselves? 12

Drugs policing? 14

Should cannabis be legalized? 16

Drugs education? 18

The benefits of medicinal drugs? 20

Are medicinal drugs safe? 22

Are we hooked on prescribed drugs? 24

Alternative drugs treatments? 26

Drugs and our future? 28

Glossary 30

Useful addresses 31

Facts to think about 31

Index 32

Drug use or abuse?

A drug is a substance that affects the way the body works, either physically or mentally. It can be man-made, or derived from plants, minerals or even animals. Most people think of drugs as illegal substances like cocaine or heroin, or legal medicines like antibiotics or painkillers, but alcohol and tobacco are also legal drugs, as are coffee and tea which contain a mild stimulant called caffeine. Some people also use everyday substances like hairspray, correction fluid, lighter fuel or glue as stimulant drugs.

Ever since human beings began experimenting with the world about them, they have used drugs for pleasure, medicine and religion. As long ago as 8000 BC native Central Americans used mescal beans as a stimulant, while Sumerian stone tablets from 4000 BC show opium being taken for calmness and pain relief. Cannabis was in use in Central Asia and China by 3000 BC.

▲ Many people from all over the world use drugs in one form or another. This picture shows a Chinese woman smoking opium.

◄ The use of drugs such as cocaine is widespread in the Western world, despite the fact that it is illegal in many countries.

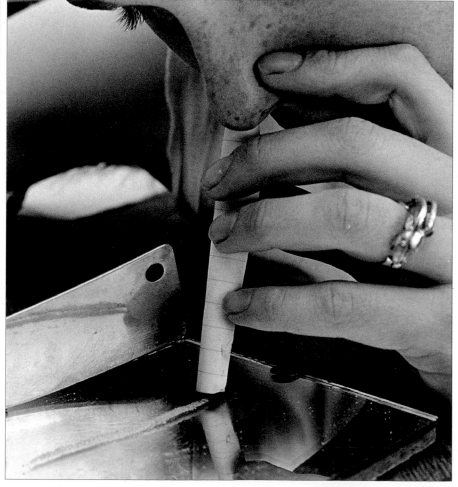

Early civilizations across the world used medicinal plants and minerals to treat disease. The Chinese, for instance, developed 16,000 remedies, many of which are still in use today. In the West the first known comprehensive list of medicines with instructions for preparation appeared in Nuremberg, Germany, in 1546; since then we have developed many thousands of drugs which have revolutionized the way doctors practise medicine.

66 I started smoking cannabis mainly because a lot of my friends were into it and I wanted to see what it was like. 99
Craig, 15

One reason why some people continue to take drugs is down to addiction. Some drugs, like heroin or crack, quickly become physically addictive, leaving the body craving more to avoid painful withdrawal symptoms. Almost any drug can cause psychological dependence when users believe they need the drug to enjoy themselves or carry on normally with their lives.

Some people are more likely to use drugs than others. The wealth and fame that come with sporting success tempts many sports stars to use anabolic steroids to enhance their strength and endurance. Canadian athlete Ben Johnson, gold medallist in the 1988 Olympics, was later disqualified for failing a drugs test. The great Argentinian footballer,

▲ *Some people take drugs because they feel they cannot cope with life. They see drug use as a way of escaping from their personal problems.*

Diego Maradona, was banned from the 1994 World Cup for taking illegal substances. But one in fifty male high school students in the US take anabolic steroids not to boost their sporting prowess, but to improve their appearance.

Those who live in the high pressure and competitive worlds of pop music and acting are particularly vulnerable – often with fatal results. In 1994 actor River Phoenix died after injecting a lethal cocktail of drugs, which he had always denied using. Sixties rock icon Jimi Hendrix was killed by an overdose at the height of his fame in 1970, while Kurt Cobain, lead singer of US rock group Nirvana, committed suicide in 1994; many people thought his death was related to his frequent use of heroin to relieve stomach pain.

66 Every band I have ever managed has had a drugs problem. And now it's getting worse. Musicians will follow the people they look up to by taking drugs. 99
Tim Collins, manager of US rock group Aerosmith

▼ *Kurt Cobain was one of many pop and rock stars who have used drugs.*

▲ *Fighting physical addiction to a drug can be very difficult as the film character Renton (played by Ewan McGregor) showed in* **Trainspotting.**

Drugs education?

◀ *These anti-drugs campaign posters from the 1990s use shocking images of users in an attempt to dissuade people from experimenting with illegal substances. Despite such campaigns, more and more people today are using drugs. This has led many to change their approach to drugs education.*

Most governments seek to control the demand for illegal drugs in two main ways: prosecuting and imprisoning those caught using them, and educating people in general about their dangers. Although some countries have increased fines and prison sentences as a deterrent against drug use, many governments now put more effort into persuading people that taking drugs can be very hazardous.

During the seventies and eighties, most drugs-education campaigns tried to scare people into steering completely clear of drugs by showing their most dangerous consequences, such as addiction or death. Many people still think that this is an effective way to cut down drug use.

66 *Fear of catastrophe, and especially of dying, is a real deterrent to very many young people. Emphasizing the dangers has kept many away from drugs.* **99**
Arnold Cragg, director of a London market research company which helps the UK government research its anti-drugs campaigns

Other drugs-education campaigns, such as Just Say No in the US, seek to give young people the skills they need to refuse offers of drugs from friends or acquaintances. The US government has also emphasized the role parents play in influencing their children about drugs.

66 *The extent to which a parent takes responsibility for their teens resisting drugs is a key factor in lowering a teen's risk of using drugs.* **99**
Joseph Califano, president, US Center on Addiction and Substance Abuse

But the rise of recreational drugs such as ecstasy during the last five years has led many people to conclude that propaganda and shock tactics simply do not work. Such campaigns, they believe, oversimplify the issue of drug abuse by branding all drugs as being equally dangerous and addictive, while failing to address the real reasons many people take drugs, such as pleasure, pressure from friends, or a desire to escape their problems.

66 Simplistic messages and sloganeering have been prominent and the dangers of drug use have often been exaggerated to the exclusion of all else in an attempt to put young people off drugs. Such an approach is fundamentally flawed. When young people eventually find out they have been lied to, they will cease to trust adult sources of drug information. 99
Julian Cohen, drugs education specialist

In recent years the emphasis in drugs education has moved towards giving young people and their parents straight facts and advice on drugs. The aim is not so much to stop people taking them, but to reduce the harm caused by their careless use. The UK government, for example, spent £6m in 1995 in training teachers and assisting drugs prevention projects to give children information on drugs from an early age.

Other countries back up drugs education with practical measures. In the Netherlands, for instance, some Amsterdam night clubs feature drugs testing labs which analyse ecstasy to assess its strength and purity in order to reduce the risk to users. Some people say this actually encourages drug use, but the Dutch have one of the lowest proportions of drug addicts – 1.6 per 100,000 people compared to 2.6 in the UK and 2.5 in France.

▲ The focus of some drugs education programmes is to give young people the skills they need to resist the pressure to take drugs from those around them. This kind of approach is most popular in the US.

▼ Children in the US taking part in a drugs-awareness programme. Some countries are now taking the approach that it is better to give young people more information about drugs and their dangers so they can make up their own minds.

Are we hooked on prescribed drugs?

Medicinal drugs are big business, and the market for developing new medicines is one of the most profitable in the world. In 1994 global sales for the pharmaceutical industry were $256 billion. The best-selling drug Zantac, for stomach ulcers, made over $3.6 billion – more than the economic output of Nepal or Jamaica.

In the Western world we depend very heavily on medicinal drugs. Most of us will take medicines of one form or another during our lives, and we expect to be able to get hold of the drugs we need to help cure or control any physical or mental problems we may have.

But some people question whether we need so many different medicines and so much of them. A seven-year survey of new drugs by the US Food and Drugs Administration found that 84 per cent make little or no contribution to existing therapies. According to the World Health Organization, two-thirds of the drugs given to children have little or no value, and that just 270 different substances are enough to meet the world's basic needs. At present, there are around 100,000 drugs available worldwide.

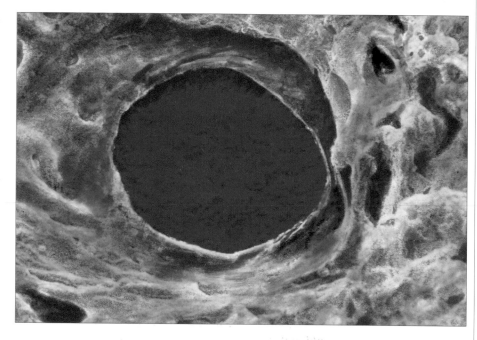

▲ A scientific photo of a stomach ulcer. Drugs can be used to deal with such medical complaints.

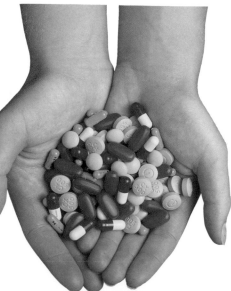

▼ There are over 100 different types of antibiotic. But do we really need so many?

Many people feel that some medicinal drugs are being overused. By the year 2000 the world had used 50,000 tons of antibiotics, designed to fight bacterial infections, yet every year we waste £9 billion by taking them unnecessarily. The overuse of these kinds of drugs has had dangerous consequences in some areas. In Pakistan, for instance, people buy antibiotics from stores without a prescription, and commonly take them for headaches. This overuse encourages bacteria to mutate into forms that are untreatable.

> *Bacteria are single-celled creatures with great genetic adaptability. Antibiotic resistant forms are now on the increase and the old medicines are not working. Even friendly bacteria have mutated into life-threatening forms.*
> *Dinyar Godrej, New Internationalist*

Since we discovered drugs like sedatives, tranquillizers and antidepressants that can alter our moods or feelings, they have become the most commonly prescribed drugs in the world, with more than five million people taking Valium in the US each year. While these drugs have helped many cope with short periods of anxiety or insomnia, prolonged use can cause addiction. By 1988, 400,000 Britons were dependent on bensodiazepines like Valium; some are now taking legal action.

> *You are told you are not addicted and you can't understand why you feel so awful if you stop taking it. So you stay on drugs year after year.*
> *42-year-old Michael Beham, addicted to Ativan for seven years*

Children can also become dependent on medicinal drugs. In the US a drug called Ritalin, used to treat attention deficit disorder (ADD) in children, is now a $350m a year industry. At the start of the 1990s Ritalin was prescribed to 500,000 children – by 2000 it was used by 9 million. While Ritalin is undoubtedly effective in helping those children with a genuine problem, some people feel that it is being prescribed to children whose problems need different solutions.

▲ *Drugs like tranquillizers calm people down and make them less anxious. However, users can quickly become reliant on them.*

▼ *Many children suffer from ADD. But are drugs always the best way of solving such problems?*

> *It's a method of social control of children. Parents want them to take the drug so they can get through the day.*
> *Dr Peter Breggin, author of Toxic Psychiatry*

Do drugs such as Ritalin and Valium actually cure problems or simply disguise them? In the UK, for instance, nearly half of mothers on low income are prescribed tranquillizers and antidepressants at some time in their lives. Some say that the drugs help them to cope with a difficult situation; others say it is often easier and cheaper for society to prescribe pills than sort out the social issues at the heart of their problems.

> *In some cases Prozac can help you struggle through, but it obviously doesn't address the cause of the depression.*
> *Dr Valerie Curran, clinical psychologist at University College, London*

Alternative drugs treatments?

The 1990s saw an explosion of interest in complementary therapies and other alternatives to drugs for treating many ailments and diseases. In the UK, for instance, 40 per cent of family doctors now refer patients for alternative therapies such as homoeopathy, osteopathy, chiropractic, acupuncture and aromatherapy. In some countries medicinal drugs are often replaced by herbal preparations – in Germany this industry turns over $2 billion a year.

Many alternative therapies have been developed over thousands of years. Most take a very different approach to disease than conventional medicine, which tends to use drugs to treat a specific symptom. Complementary therapies usually aim to treat the person as whole, taking into account their physical, mental and emotional state, and boosting general health in order to prevent the onset of disease.

66 *Medicine has tended to make illness an engineering job. But illness is made up of experience or symptoms. The person who suffers those experiences has been left to one side.* 99
Simon Mills, Exeter University Centre for Complementary Health

▲ *A patient receiving treatment by moxibustion, a form of the alternative therapy acupuncture.*

▼ *A herbal treatment being prepared. Some scientists are doubtful about their effectiveness.*

But many doctors and scientists are still very sceptical about alternative therapies. They often say that any benefits are 'all in the mind' of the patient and that the cures have no basis in science. Therapists and their supporters, however, say that this is a very narrow-minded view.

66 *The Western scientific approach is a closed system of rules which . . . claims to be the only acceptable, universal approach. It has narrowed our conceptions of health and disease to biology, separating the individual from the wider environment.* 99
Dinyar Godrej, New Internationalist

In an increasing number of cases science is beginning to back up the claims of alternative therapists. A study recently found that extracts of St John's Wort, plants widely used in folk medicine, in particular to treat depression, is as effective as synthetic antidepressants and has fewer side-effects. In some countries this is already accepted – in Germany in 2000 the remedy outsold Prozac by 20:1.

But avoiding drug treatment involves more than just finding an alternative. Doctors recommend that we try to avoid disease in the first place by leading healthier lifestyles, pointing out that poor diets and lack of exercise can lead to a range of health problems like heart disease, high blood pressure and back pain. In 1996 the World Health Organization launched a global campaign to combat obesity, which accounts for nearly 10% of all health-care costs in Western countries. It is predicted that, if present trends continue, the entire population of the US will be obese by 2230.

▼ *Obesity is a widespread problem in the Western world today. Should we be encouraging people to lead healthier lifestyles?*

▲ *The terrible conditions that many are forced to live in are responsible for much of the world's illness and our reliance on medicinal drugs.*

However, the best way to cut down on global drug treatment would be to tackle the world's most common and deadly disease – poverty. Half the world's population is too poor to buy even essential drugs, and their health is undermined by lack of food, clean drinking water, housing and good sanitation. Less than 4 per cent of medical research money worldwide goes into finding treatment for diseases prevalent in the developing world, where three-quarters of the world's population live and die.

66 *Every year in the developing world 12.2 million children under five die, most of them from causes which could have been prevented for just a few US cents per child. They die largely because of world indifference but most of all they die because they are poor.* 99
World Health Organization

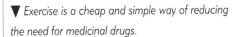

▼ *Exercise is a cheap and simple way of reducing the need for medicinal drugs.*

Drugs and our future?

We may have over 100,000 medicinal drugs at our disposal, but the medicinal drugs industry sees room for plenty more.

66 More than half the world's illnesses have no medicines. The world's population continues to age. There's still plenty of growth to come. 99
Jean Rene Fourtou, head of pharmaceutical giant Rhône-Poulenc

Scientists are currently working on new drugs to cure diseases such as cancer, arthritis and Aids. In the area of cancer, for example, which affects one in three people in the UK alone, the medical establishment predicts a revolution in treatment over the next 25 years which will cut deaths by a third.

66 For those who do develop cancer, we are now starting a new golden age of drug discovery. . . Some of these new designer drugs are already in early trials, and we shall see many more such trials starting over the next ten years. 99
Professor Karol Sikora,
deputy director of clinical research, the Imperial Cancer Research Fund

In the future doctors also hope to produce drugs that only affect the parts of the body where they are needed, which could reduce or eliminate unpleasant or dangerous side-effects. At present, anti-cancer drugs, for instance, make people feel very ill as they kill normal cells as well as tumour cells; future cancer therapies may home in on just the cancer cells, leaving healthy cells untouched.

▶ Despite the number of medicinal drugs already on the market, there is still no treatment available for Aids. In this picture, a scientist works on a vaccine for the disease.

▼ At the present rate of scientific advance, many other diseases, including cancer and arthritis, could soon become things of the past, according to some researchers.

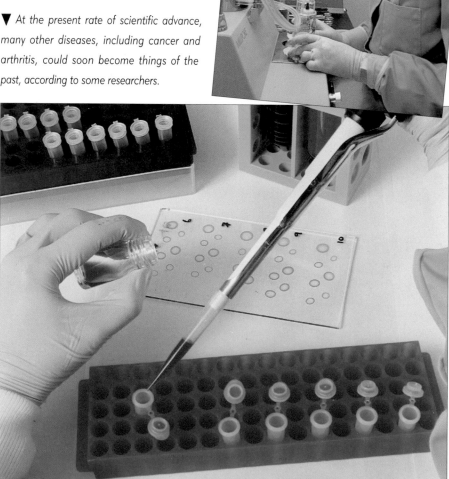

But scientists do not intend to stop at finding cures for common diseases. Some predict that within ten years 'smart' drugs will improve memory, learning and intelligence, even ward off mental decay in old age. We may have drugs which control our weight, even drugs that reduce the speed at which we age. Scientists are also working on drug treatments for violent people. Such drugs would raise our levels of seratonin – the chemical in the brain which helps to inhibit aggression.

Some people believe that medical science may also hold the answer for the problem of illegal drug abuse. Scientists are currently testing a cocaine vaccine on human volunteers which may be the forerunner to a new generation of inoculations to cure drug addiction.

▲ *This man eventually died of Aids as a result of injecting drugs with an infected needle. Will science solve the problem of drug abuse?*

▼ *In the future, drugs may also help us live longer. Would this necessarily be a good thing?*

These vaccines are intended to work by prompting the body to produce antibodies to substances like cocaine, so the drug no longer has any effect when taken.

But do we actually need most of these 'designer' drugs? Do we need drugs to alter our every mood or change our biological inheritance? Are we getting close to the situation portrayed in Aldous Huxley's novel *Brave New World*, where everyone takes drugs to find tranquillity?

66 *Tranquillizers do not change our environment, nor do they change our personalities. They merely reduce our responsiveness to stimuli. Once the response has been dulled, the irritating surface noise of living muted or eliminated, the spark and brilliance are also gone.* 99
Indra Devi, yoga practitioner

Glossary

ACUPUNCTURE A Chinese therapy involving piercing of the skin with needles to treat various illnesses.

ADDICTION A physical or mental dependency on a habit or substance; a strong desire to repeat taking drugs.

ALCOHOL A legal depressant drug.

AMPHETAMINE Also known as speed or whizz. A man-made stimulant drug which can come in powder or tablet form.

ANABOLIC STEROIDS Substances similar to the body's hormones which control growth and development.

ANAESTHETIC A drug which takes away feeling in some part of the body or renders the patient unconscious.

ANTIBIOTICS Drugs which kill off the bacteria which lead to infection.

ANTIDEPRESSANT A type of drug used to treat depression.

AROMATHERAPY A therapy that uses perfumed oils and massage to treat patients.

ARTHRITIS A painful disease affecting the joints of the body.

CAFFEINE A mild stimulant found in coffee, tea, cola drinks and chocolate.

CANNABIS Also known as marijuana, blow, grass, dope, weed and pot. A drug made from the *Cannabis sativa* plant which usually comes as dried leaves or in an oily block.

CARTEL A group of people or companies who cooperate together in the same business.

CHIROPRACTIC A method of healing which involves gentle manipulation to treat disorders of the joints and muscles.

COCAINE Also known as coke or snow. A strong stimulant drug which comes in powder form.

CONTRACEPTIVE PILL A hormone-based drug which prevents pregnancy.

CRACK Also known as base or rock, crack is a crystalline form of cocaine which is usually smoked.

DEPRESSANT A type of drug that slows down the functioning of the body.

ECSTASY Also known as E, doves and MDMA. A synthetic drug with stimulant and hallucinogenic effects which comes in tablet form.

HALLUCINOGENIC A type of drug which alters the way we see and hear things.

HEROIN Also known as smack, gear or skag, heroin is a powder made from the opium poppy. A depressant drug which is usually injected but can also be smoked.

HOMOEOPATHY A therapy that uses tiny amounts of natural substances to treat disease.

LSD Also known as acid, LSD (lysergic acid) is a hallucinogenic drug made from a fungus. It is usually dropped on to paper, but also comes as tablets or capsules.

MAGIC MUSHROOMS A variety of small, bell-shaped fungi. They are usually eaten raw and produce a hallucinogenic effect.

MULTIPLE SCLEROSIS A nerve disorder which often gradually leads to paralysis and death.

NICOTINE A powerful and highly poisonous drug. It is the main chemical responsible for the addictive quality of cigarettes.

OBESITY A condition of extreme over-weight.

OPIUM A heroin-type drug which is derived directly from the opium poppy.

OSTEOPATHY A treatment which involves working on the physical structure of the body using massage, manipulation and stretching.

PHARMACEUTICAL INDUSTRY The research, testing, manufacture and sale of medicinal drugs.

PNEUMONIA A serious inflammation of the lungs that can lead to death.

STIMULANT A type of drug which increases energy or concentration.

TOBACCO The main ingredient in cigarettes. Contains the drug nicotine.

TRAFFICKING To supply or smuggle drugs within and across different countries.

TRANQUILLIZERS Drugs used to treat anxiety, depression and insomnia.

TUBERCULOSIS A highly infectious disease of the lungs.

VACCINE A substance injected into the body to protect against disease.

WITHDRAWAL SYMPTOMS The effects felt when a user goes without a drug for some time.